The Resistance Tubing Handbook

Written By

Andre Noel Potvin
Michael Jespersen

Edited By

EXPERT: STRENGTH TRAINING & GENERAL FITNESS
Andre Noel Potvin
MSC, CSCS, CES

EXPERT: STRENGTH AND CONDITIONING & FITNESS
Bill Luke
PhD, CSCS, Registered Kinesiologist

EXPERT: STRETCHING & GENERAL FITNESS

GENERAL EDITOR
Michael Jespersen
COPY EDITOR
Karl Thorson

Eleventh Printing
(January 2011)

Consult your physician before starting any exercise program. This is of particular importance if you are over 35 and have been inactive for a period of time. The author and publisher disclaim any liability from loss, injury, or damage, personal or otherwise, resulting from the procedures in this book.

Productive Fitness Products Inc.
18525 53rd. Avenue, Unit 120
Surrey, B.C. V3S 7A4

Productive Fitness Publishing Inc.
1645 Jill's Court, Suite 102
Bellingham, WA 98226

E-mail: info@productivefitness.com

Visit our Website: www.productivefitness.com

Jespersen, Michael, 1962-
The great stretch tubing handbook

ISBN 0-9696773-6-7
1. Exercise. 2. Stretch Tubing. I. Potvin, Andre Noel, 1961. II. Thorson, Karl, 1964- III. Title
GV481.J47 1999 613.7'1 C99-910995-2

Table of Contents

Introduction

If you do a lot of travelling, or are looking for a method of exercise that is lightweight, inexpensive and takes up little space, then resistance tubing is for you. Long used in physical therapy and rehabilitation, resistance tubing offers a means of strength training that emphasizes both eccentric and concentric contraction of the muscles. In other words, like working with weights, you have resistance in both the beginning phase of the exercise and the return phase of the exercise. Studies have shown that a significant benefit is achieved by resisting the pull on the return phase of the exercise.

The secret of successful resistance training is to constantly challenge your muscles by increasing the resistance level, number of repetitions or sets. Also known as progressive resistance, because you are continually demanding more work from your muscles, they are forced to adapt by getting stronger. Most tubing manufacturers make several levels of resistance: the thicker the tube, the more the resistance. Each level of resistance is designated by a different color. The colors are not standardized from manufacturer to manufacturer, but as a general guideline the lighter colors are lighter resistance and the darker colors are heavier resistance.

Types of tubing vary, but it is best to purchase tubing specifically designed for exercise, ideally with handles. This will make workouts a lot easier and safer. Tubing is not designed for heavy strength training/bodybuilding, but rather to tone and define your muscles through high repetition exercises or to complement an already existing weight-training routine. Additionally, if you have sustained an injury, tubing will allow you to exercise with a light resistance so you can gradually increase the muscle's strength.

One of the great benefits of tubing is its simplicity. You don't need a lot of accessories to get a good workout. One accessory you will need is a door attachment. Unfortunately, door attachments are difficult to find at the retail level, even though some tubing manufacturers offer them. Fortunately, it is quite simple to make our own attachment with some soft, thin nylon cord.

Good luck and congratulations on using this exceptional fitness training tool.

Rubberized Resistance

There are basically two options for rubberized resistance: tubing and stretch bands. As a rule, tubing is better-suited to exercise because it is more durable and the handles are pre-attached. Handles can be purchased separately for stretch bands, which also allows you to adjust the length. Both tubing and stretch bands wear down over time and with exposure to heat and cold, so check them often for damage and replace them when necessary. In general, however, all the exercises can be done with either tubing or stretch bands, depending on your preference.

Some of the advantages and disadvantages of using rubber resistance tools are:

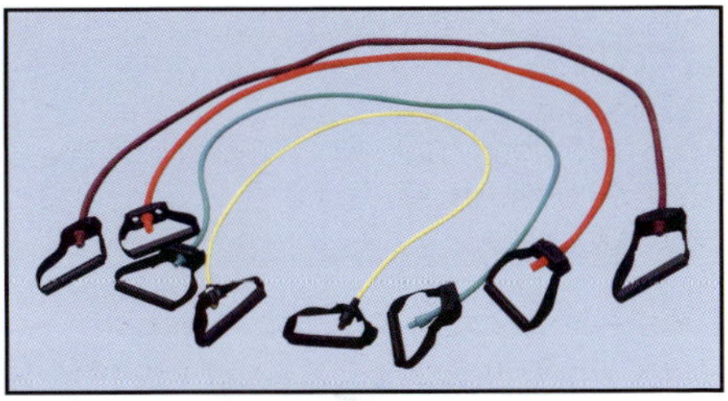

Resistance tubing

Stretch Band

Advantages

- Lightweight and portable
- Takes up little space
- Resistance on both concentric & eccentric contraction
- Can be attached at different height levels to create exercises difficult to reproduce with free weights.

Disadvantages

- As the tubing is stretched, the resistance gets greater; thus, the greatest resistance is at the mid-point of an exercise when the tubing is at its most stretched point. This may not be the target muscle's greatest point of strength nor the most efficient biomechanical position.
- There is no method for gauging exactly the resistance level of an exercise. Therefore, trying to increase resistance incrementally can be difficult.

Muscle Diagrams

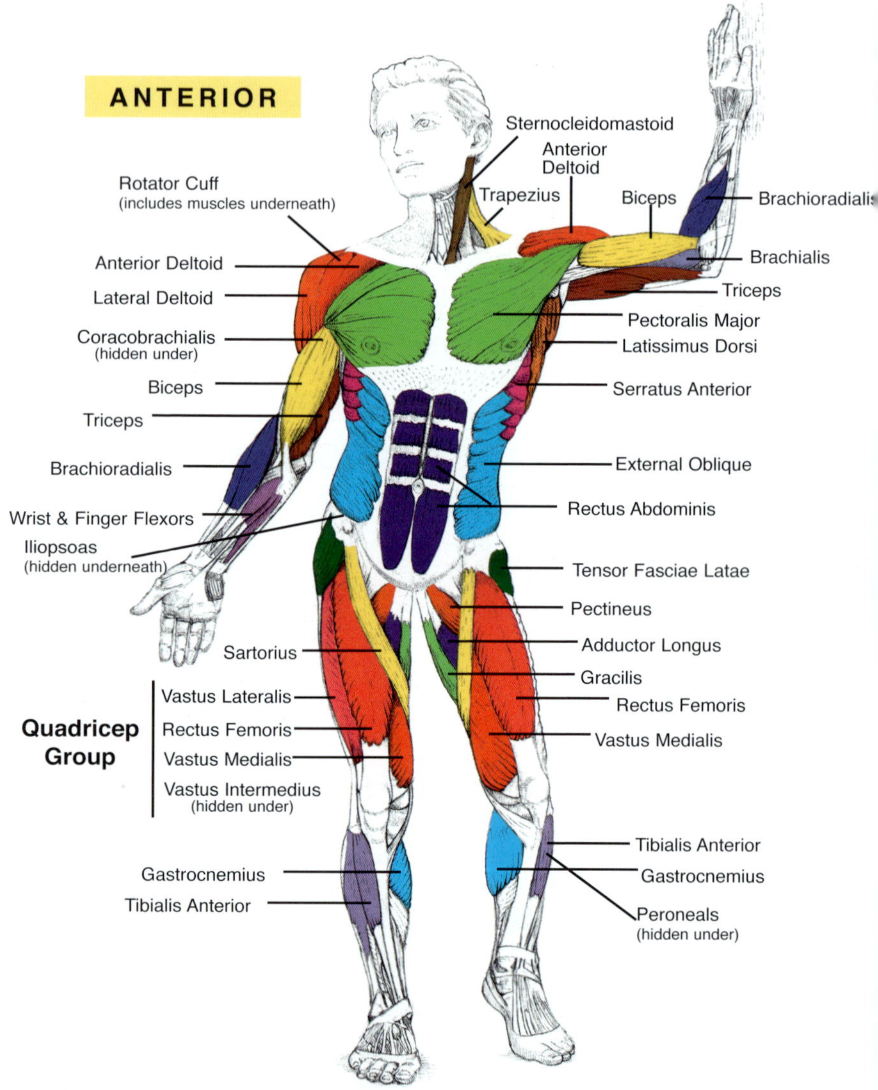

Neck Extensors	upper trapezius, illiocotalis cervicis, longissimus cervicis, spinalis cervicis. **Deep Extensors**: semispinalis cervicis, spinalis cervicis
Neck Retractors	longus colli, longus capitus
Scapular Depressors	latissimus dorsi, low trapezius
Scapular Retractors	rhomboids, mid-low trapezius
Shoulder Stabilizers	pectoralis major, deltoid, triceps (long head), latissimus dorsi, teres major, rotator cuff
Core (outer unit)	rectus abdominus, erector spinae, internal and external obliques
Core (inner unit)	pelvic floor muscles, diaphragm, multifidui, levator ani, transversus abdominus

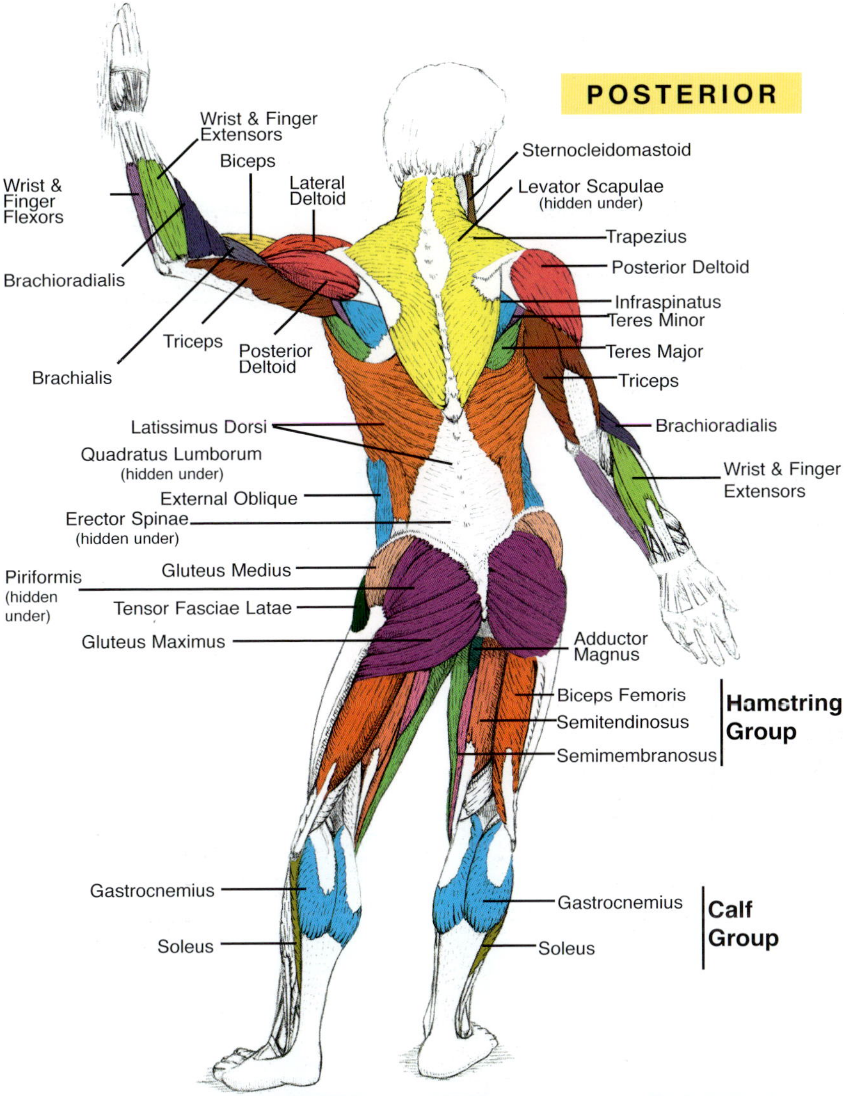

Pelvis Stabilizers	rectus abdominus, obliques, quadratus lumborum, latissimus dorsi
Spinal Rotators	obliques, erector spinae (unilaterally), rectus abdominus (unilaterally), deep spinal rotators
Hip Stabilizers	hip flexors, hip abductors, hip extensors, hip rotators
Hip Flexors	iliopsoas, sartorius, rectus femoris, tensor facia latae
Hip Adductors	adductor brevis, longus and magnus, gracilis, pectineus
Hip Extensors	gluteus maximus, hamstrings
Hip Abductors	gluteus medius and minimus, tensor fasciae latae, piriformis
Ankle Stabilizers	gastrocnemius, soleus, tibialis posterior, tibialis anterior, peroneals, extensor digitorum longus, brevis

How to Make and Use a Door Attachment

How to Make a Door Strap

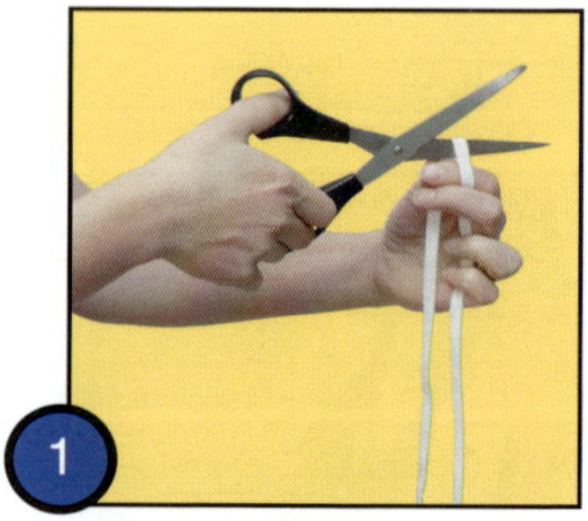

Using a thin, soft nylon cord, cut a piece 5 ft (60 inches) in length. (Or you can use a 54" white athletic shoelace.)

Using a thin, soft nylon cord, cut a piece 5 ft (60 inches) in length. (Or you can use a 54" white athletic shoelace.)

Fold the cord in half again, gripping the ends between your thumb and forefinger.

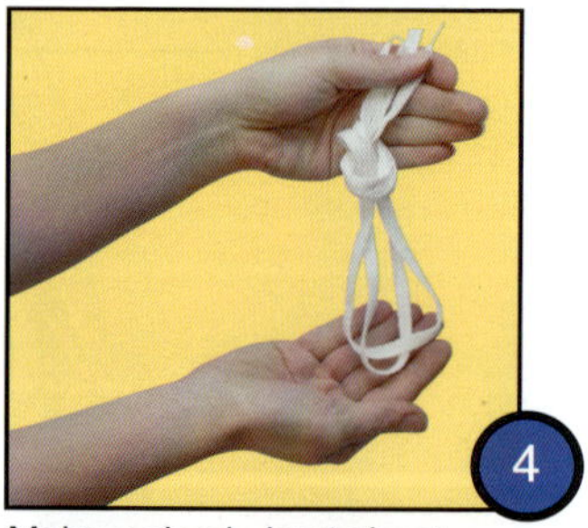

Make a simple knot about 1/3 of the way down from the ends.

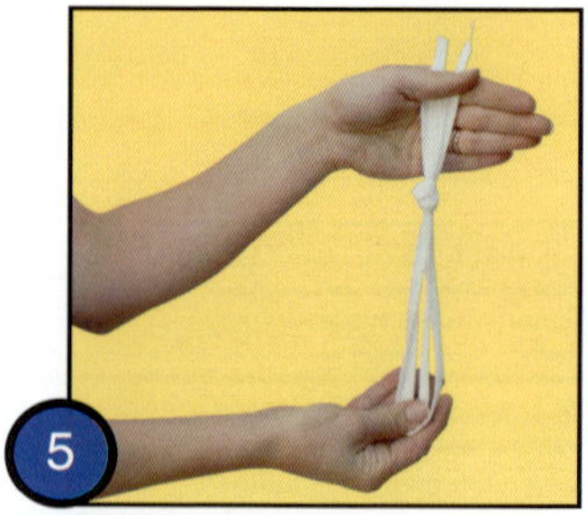

Tighten.

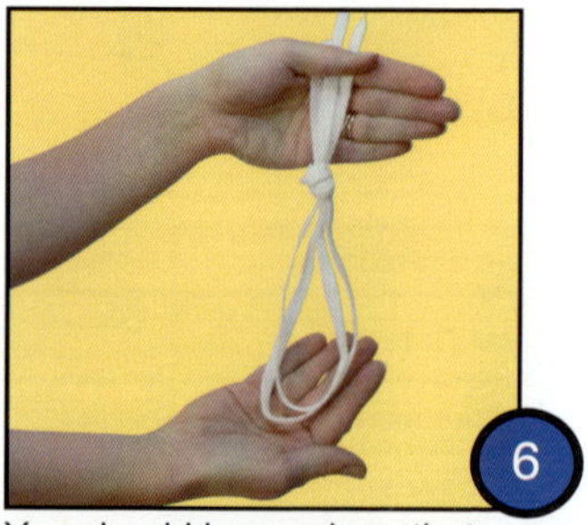

You should have a loop that takes up about 2/3 of the length.

How to attach strap to tubing

1

At exactly the midpoint of the tubing, make a small loop in your right hand. Thread the loop of the strap part-way through the loop of the tubing. Spread the strap loop apart with your left hand.

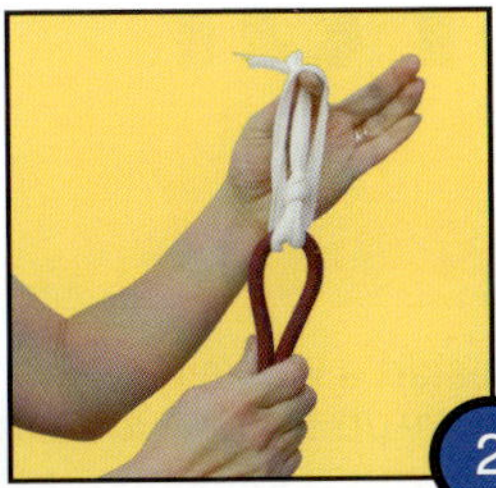

2

Fold the knotted end of the strap over the tubing and feed it through the strap loop.

Pull tight.

How to Attach Strap to Door

1

With the door open, feed knotted end of the door strap between the door frame and the door. Always use the hinged side of the door: hinged side has more stability.

2

Shut the door, so it is tight, making sure the latch catches. The knot of the strap must be completely through to the other side of the door. MAKE SURE THE DOOR IS COMPLETELY SHUT AND LOCKED BEFORE STARTING AN EXERCISE.

General Guidelines

- **Always warm up before you start a workout.**
  Try to do a total body warm-up before you start training. A good example of a total body warmup is using a rowing or skiing machine. It is especially important to warm up the specific muscle groups you are going to be using. This can be as simple as performing a warm-up set of high repetitions and light resistance for each exercise.
- **Use proper posture.**
  Maintaining proper posture will greatly reduce chances of injury and maximize exercise benefit. When standing, always keep your feet shoulder-width apart, unless otherwise suggested. Do not lock your knees: it puts an unnecessary strain on them. Keep your back flat and straight, making sure not to twist or arch it in order to complete an exercise.
- **Use proper form.**
  Focus on the proper motion of the exercise, while concentrating on the specific muscles being used. Do not sacrifice proper form to do heavier resistance or perform more repetitions. Keeping proper form also means moving in a smooth fluid motion. Know when your muscles are too tired to keep going.
- **Breathe properly.**
  Never hold your breath during any part of an exercise. Holding your breath may cause severe intra-thoracic pressure and raise blood pressure leading to dizziness, blackout or worse! The rule of thumb is to exhale slowly on exertion and inhale on the return part of the exercise.
- **Stop training if you feel pain.**
  If you feel pain during a specific exercise, stop immediately. Any continuation may aggravate an existing injury. Reevaluate your routine to make sure you are doing a proper warm-up. Decrease the amount of resistance you are using. Talk to a recognized health professional.
- **Frequency.**
  Exercise each muscle group 2-3 times per week. Allow a minimum of 48 hours rest for each muscle group worked. If you are doing a total body workout, three training sessions per week, performed on every second day, is adequate.
- **Duration.**
  A weight training routine should take anywhere from 45 minutes to 1 hour to complete. Add another 20 to 60 minutes if you are including aerobics.
- **Fatigue.**
  Try to fatigue your muscles within the suggested rep range. Fatigue is when you can't possibly do another rep without sacrificing form.
- **Range of Motion.**
  Moving through a complete range of motion (ROM) allows the muscle to stretch before contraction and increases the number of fibers being recruited. This produces maximum contraction and force. By working the full ROM, flexibility will be maintained or even increased.

- **Speed of Movement.**
  Exercise movements should be slow and controlled. The start phase of the exercise should take 2-3 seconds and the return phase 3-4 seconds Do not use momentum to complete an exercise. Momentum puts unnecessary stress on tendons, ligaments, and joints and does not develop increased strength.
- **Proper Form.**
  Focus on the proper motion of the exercise, while concentrating on the specific muscles being used. Do not sacrifice proper form to use a heavier resistance or perform more repetitions.
- **Change Routine.**
  If you want to make changes in the exercises you do, wait until about the six-week point.
- **Rest Interval.**
  Allow a brief pause (30 to 60 seconds) between sets to give the muscles a chance to partially recover before working them again.

Torso Stabilization

Torso stabilization is the process of tightening the "core" muscles around your spine to protect you from injury during any lifting, pushing or pulling movements. The core muscles are grouped into two units; the inner core and the outer core (page 7). Both units need to contract in a co-ordinated manner to provide maximum protection and performance.

Why is it so important to learn this technique?
Torso stabilization is essential since the spine acts as the body's anchor from which all other muscles pull in order to effectively function. Without this muscle and spine co-ordinated effort, the risk of injury is high. Worse, our lack of fitness, combined with the degeneration processes of aging and also a poor understanding of how to tighten the core can be a recipe for disaster.

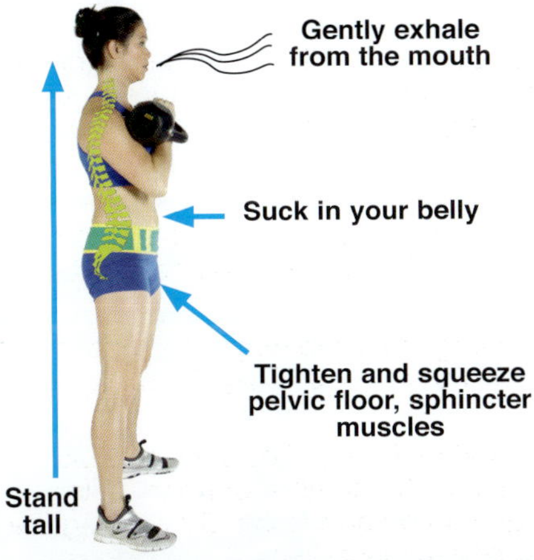

Think of the core as creating a cylinder-like squeeze around your spine. As you contract this cylinder, all sides of the muscular walls close in together to enhance the compression force and support of your spine.

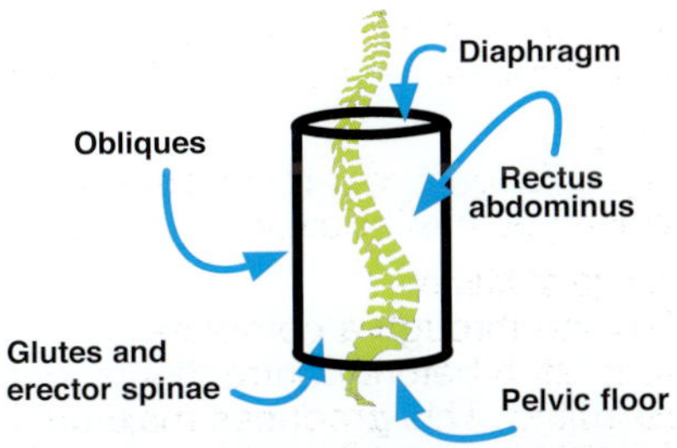

Sample Routine

REPETITIONS, SETS AND WORKLOAD

Repetitions: Are the number of times an exercise is done consecutively without rest.
Set: One complete series of continuous, consecutive repetitions is called a Set.
Workload: Refers to the amount of weight used in working a particular muscle or muscle group.

Exercise	Bodypart	Reps*	Sets	Workload
Chest Flye	Chest	12-15	2	*
Decline Chest Press	Chest	12-15	2	*
Standing High Pulldown	Back	12-15	2	*
Half Superman	Back	12-15	2	*
Forward Shoulder Press	Shoulder	12-15	2	*
Standing Bicep Curl	Biceps	12-15	2	*
Overhead Tricep Extension	Triceps	12-15	2	*
Standing Side Bend	Core	12-15	2	*
Crunch	Core	12-15	2	*
Squat	Legs	12-15	2	*

The workload is determined by finding the resistance level that causes your muscles to fatigue within the given number of reps. Fatigue is best defined as the point where you can't possibly do one more repetition without sacrificing proper form. Resistance levels are determined by the thickness of the tube, as well as the length of the tubing you have to work with. The shorter and/or thicker the tubing, the more the resistance.
It is a good idea to make notes on each exercise so that you can duplicate the resistance level (or slightly increase) during the next workout.

Training Tip:

A great way to record and track your routine is to keep a journal be sure to check out our "Ultimate Weight Training Journal" available instores and online.

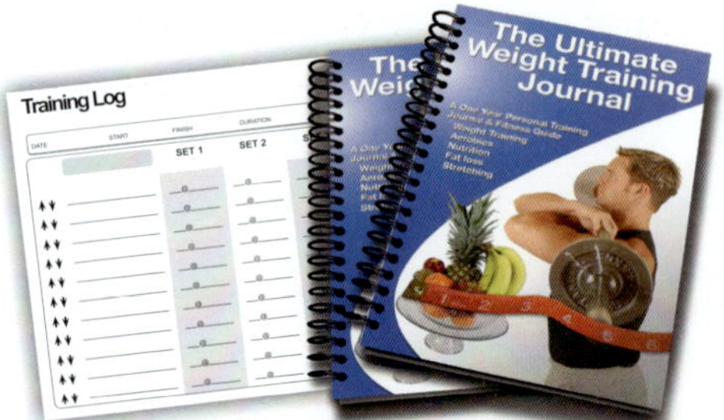

Resistance Tubing Safety

- When using the door attachment, make sure the door is **securely closed** and **locked** to prevent sudden opening.
- Inspect the tubing for nicks, worn spots, cuts or other malformations prior to each workout by holding the tubing to the light and by running your thumb and forefinger along the surface to feel for any inconsistencies. Pay particular attention to the area where the tubing and door attachment meet.
- If tubing is found to be damaged, discontinue use and replace it **immediately**.
- Avoid leaning into an exercise. For safety reasons you do not want to get caught off-balance should the tubing snap or door open suddenly. By properly spacing your legs and bending at the knees, you should be able to achieve the necessary stability to properly perform the exercise.
- Wear proper exercise footwear. Never wear golf shoes or cleats when using tubing.
- Never attach the tubing to any device that may be unsecured or unstable.
- Use tubes and bands specifically designed for exercise.
- Be prepared to replace tubing when it shows signs of degeneration.
- Keep tubing away from heat, cold, and sharp objects.
- Avoid prolonged exposure to sunlight or water.
- Never pull the tubing directly towards your face.
- Only one person should use the tubing when performing an exercise.
- Never tie two pieces of rubber tubing together.
- Keep tubing and accessories away from young children.
- Never resistance tubing more than three times its resting length.

Safe Exercise Flow Chart
(Soreness Test)

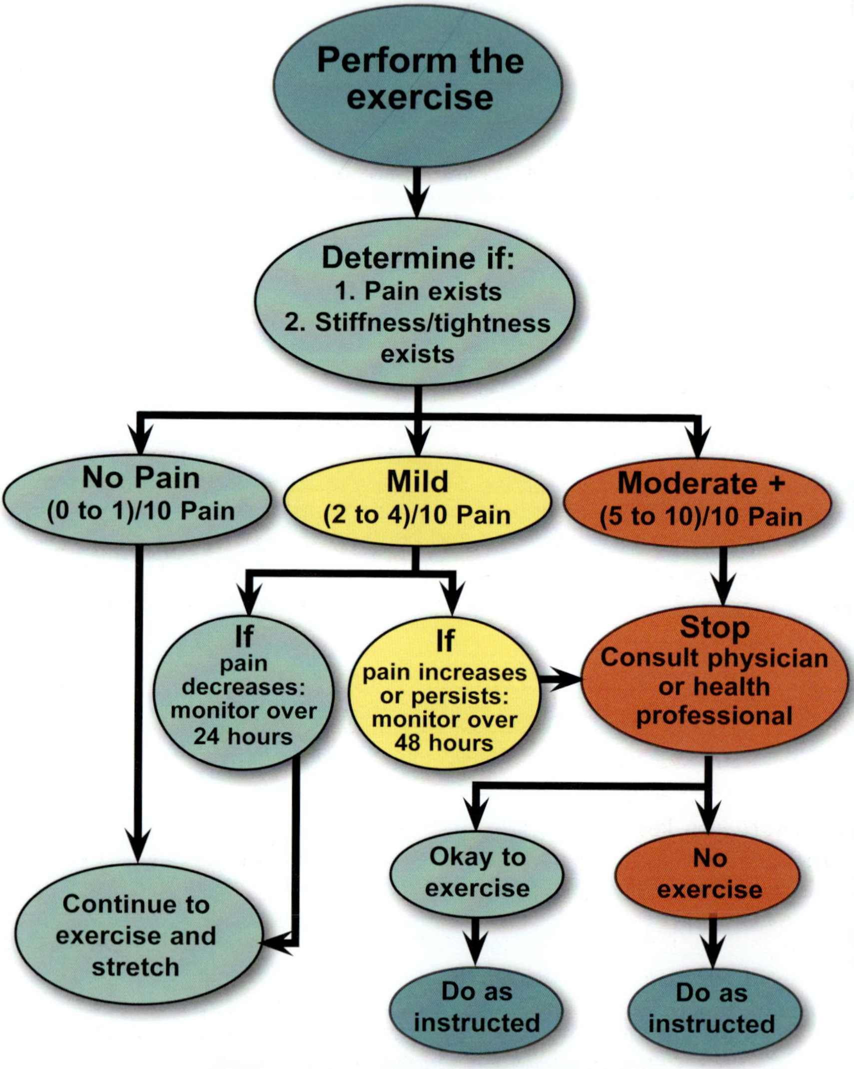

Pain Reference Scale
out of Ten

0 = No Pain.
3 = Does not affect normal movement.
5 = Affects normal movement.
10 = Extreme pain.

Stretching

By Andre Noel Potvin, MSc, CSCS, CES

Why Stretch?

Regular stretching helps maintain and improve flexibility. The definition of flexibility is a joint's ability to move through a normal range of motion (ROM). Each joint has its own degree of flexibility; therefore, it's possible to be very flexible in one joint and stiff in another. The primary limitation in joint ROM is due to the tough connective tissue running through the muscle belly. Other factors that influence flexibility include:

- age
- genetics
- activity (previous exercise experience)
- joint structure (injury or no injury)
- gender (women are generally more flexible than men)
- body temperature (slightly warmer than normal is more effective)
- opposing muscle tightness (opposing muscles are responsible for returning limbs to their original position).

Stretching is the practice of tissue elongation, or lengthening muscle and connective tissue for the purpose of reducing tension around a specific joint. Stretching allows the joint to move more freely. Some benefits of stretching include:

- increased joint range of motion
- reduced joint stress due to muscular imbalances
- reduced chronic soft-tissue pain (i.e., neck, back, knees, etc.)
- increased relaxation
- enhanced well-being

When stretching, keep the following points in mind.

- Stretch to a mild-intensity (30%-40% of maximum intensity). The stretch should feel like a comfortable pull.
- Hold stretches for 30-60 seconds, until the muscle relaxes. When you begin a stretch, your muscles will feel tight; this feeling subsides as the muscle relaxes, then elongates.
- Stretch when your muscles are warm, ideally after physical activity, such as resistance training or aerobics. Stretching with warm muscles enhances results. Avoid stretching cold muscles.
- Pay extra attention to your tightest joints. Flexibility is joint-specific; focus on all joints with restricted ROM.
- Proper body alignment is critical for getting maximum results. Carefully study and follow the stretch positions and explanations in this handbook.
- Repeat each stretch 2-3 times.
- Breathe deeply as you stretch; this enhances relaxation by stimulating the Central Nervous System (CNS).

Flexibility Training Guidelines

Intensity	• Using a scale of 1-10, stretch at about a 3-4 intensity level (1=very mild stretch, and 10=extreme stretch). You should feel a comfortable pulling sensation, never pain. 1 out of 10= very very mild 5 out of 10= invokes pain 10 out of 10= extremely intense
Time	• Hold each stretch for 30-60 seconds. • Perform each stretch 2-3 times.
Other Variables	• For optimal results, stretch after a warm-up or aerobic activity when the muscles are warm.

IMPORTANT SAFETY TIPS

- STOP stretching if you feel pain.
- NEVER push against or force a joint beyond its limit.
- NEVER hold a stretch longer than 90 seconds. Doing so could weaken the tissue and increase the risk of injury and/or irritation.
- 5 or more on 10 invokes pain and should never be done to improve flexibility. This will cause a muscle to contract and not relax defeating the purpose of the stretch.

Stretching Routine

Neck Retractions/Chin Tucks

(Stretches: Neck extensors)

- In a standing position, poke your chin and head forward, then draw your chin backward, flattening the back of your neck.
- Keeping neck retracted (chin in), tuck chin down, toward your chest.
- Hold for 30-60 seconds; repeat 2-3 times Repeat often during the day.

Head Tilts

(Stretches: Scalenes, Upper trapezius)

- Tilt head to the right and lower your left shoulder.
- Place right hand on left side of head to gently intensify stretch.
- Hold for 30-60 seconds; repeat 2-3 times. Switch sides.

Caution: Be very gentle when intensifying this stretch.

Head Turn

(Stretches: Neck rotators)

- Place right index and middle finger on left side of jaw.
- Place left hand on back of head, on the right side.
- Gently rotate head to the right, using hands to intensify stretch.
- Hold for 30-60 seconds; repeat 2-3 times. Switch sides.

Ball Arch

(Stretches: Chest, Ribs, Shoulders, Abs, Spine)

- Lie face-up on a stability ball.
- Place hands behind head, holding abs tight.
- Squeeze shoulder blades together, opening elbows to the side.
- Arch your back over the ball with feet flat on floor, keeping neck neutral as you slightly look up toward ceiling.
- Breathe deeply, expanding the chest.
- Start by holding for 5 seconds, then releasing. Gradually increase over time to hold for 30-60 seconds; repeat 2-3 times.

Handcuff Towel

(Stretches: Anterior deltoid, Chest, Biceps)

- Hold a towel behind your back with palms facing body.
- Squeeze shoulder blades together and pull arms backward.
- Keep abs tight and don't arch lower back.
- Hold for 30-60 seconds; repeat 2-3 times.

Note: Avoid leaning forward, rolling shoulders forward or poking your neck forward.

Advanced: Grip fingers together and repeat as above without the towel.

Overhead Reach

(Stretches: Latissimus dorsi)

- Standing or kneeling, interlace fingers and reach arms overhead, palms down.
- Keep neck neutral; avoid poking head forward.
- Hold for 30-60 seconds; repeat 2-3 times.

Variation: Clasp the left wrist, pulling arm up and to the right. Repeat on left.

Variation

Seated Arm Cross-Over Hug

(Stretches: Rhomboids, Middle and lower trapezius, Erector spinae)

- Sit with legs slightly bent in front of you.
- Cross arms, keeping them straight; hold right thigh with left hand and left thigh with right hand.
- Sit back, using your abs.
- Hold for 30-60 seconds; repeat 2-3 times.

Shoulder Towel Stretch

(Bottom arm stretch– External rotators, Anterior deltoid)
(Top arm stretch - Posterior deltoid, Triceps)

- Hold one end of towel in right hand, raising right arm overhead.
- With towel hanging behind back, grab other end with left hand.
- Pull up on towel with right hand, straightening arm, to stretch left (bottom) shoulder.
- Pull down on towel with left hand, straightening arm, to stretch right (top) shoulder.
- Hold for 30-60 seconds; repeat 2-3 times. Switch sides.

Note: Keep shoulder blades squeezed together.

Bottom arm stretch   Top arm stretch

Single-Knee Corkscrew

(Stretches: Gluteus maximus, Obliques, Erector spinae, Piriformis)

- Sit with left leg straight and right leg bent, knee close to chest and right foot on opposite side of left knee.
- Place right hand on floor behind you for support.
- Wrap left arm around right knee, pulling up into left shoulder.
- Rotate torso until you feel a comfortable stretch.
- Breathe deeply. As you exhale, twist a little more.
- Hold for 30-60 seconds; repeat 2-3 times. Switch sides.

Note: This stretch works best when you sit up as straight as possible.

Runner's Hip Stretch

(Stretches: Tensor fasciae latae, Iliopsoas, Rectus femoris, Obliques, Erector spinae, Spine)

- Take a large step forward with right leg.
- Place a stability ball under right buttock for support, keeping most of your weight on legs.
- Bend left knee down and toward front leg.
- Twist torso to the right, placing right hand on ball (or right buttock), and left hand on right side of right thigh.
- Squeeze buttocks and tilt pelvis forward. (Imagine pelvis is a bucket tilting to pour water behind you.)
- You should feel the stretch in the left hip and thigh.

Hold for 30-60 seconds; repeat 2-3 times. Switch sides.

Note: Avoid arching lower back

Advanced: Cross left foot behind you and to the right; repeat as above.

Variation

Seated Towel Stretch

(Stretches: Hamstrings, Gastrocnemius)

- Sit with both legs slightly bent in front of you.
- Wrap a towel or rope around left foot.
- Gently straighten left leg until you feel a comfortable stretch.
- Pull left toes and foot toward you.

Hold for 30-60 seconds; repeat 2-3 times. Switch sides.

Note: Lift chest and straighten back by arching through lower back; retract shoulder blades (avoid rounding them forward) and keep neck neutral, or look slightly down.

Bent-Knee Stretch

(Stretches: Quadriceps, Hip flexors)

- Hold left ankle while standing.
- Pull left heel to buttocks, or until you reach a comfortable stretch.
- Point left knee toward floor.
- Tilt pelvis. (Imagine pelvis is a bucket tilting to pour water behind you.)
- Keep spine straight and upright, chest lifted and head neutral.

Hold for 30-60 seconds; repeat 2-3 times. Switch sides.

Modification: For a stiff knee or quadriceps, place left foot on a bench or chair.

Variation

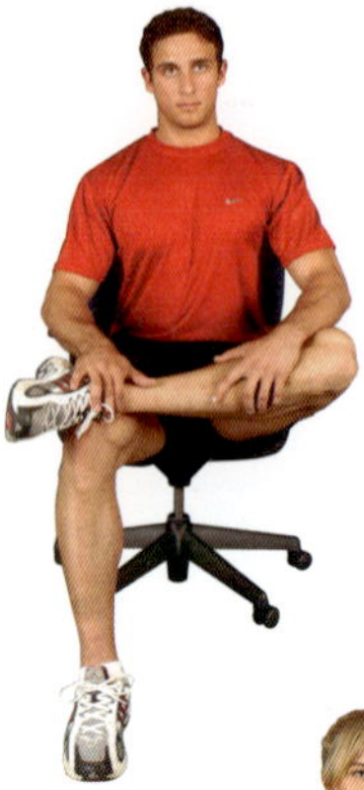

Cross-Leg Stretch

(Stretches: Gluteus medius and minimus)

- Sit on a chair or bench and cross left leg so left ankle rests on right knee.
- Sit straight with chest lifted and shoulder blades slightly squeezed together.
- Gently press on left knee with left hand until you feel a comfortable stretch.
- Hold for 30-60 seconds; repeat 2-3 times. Switch sides.

Inner Thigh Stretch

(Stretches: Adductors)

- Stand with feet wide apart, both hands on left thigh.
- Perform a slight squat, leading with buttocks and keeping chest lifted.
- Shift your weight to the left until you feel a comfortable stretch.
- Angle left foot a little toward the left, with left knee aligned over second toe.
- Point right foot forward, keeping sole flat on floor.
- Hold for 30-60 seconds; repeat 2-3 times. Switch sides.

Bent-Knee Calf Stretch

(Stretches: Soleus)

- Step forward with right foot, placing right heel on floor, toes up and both hands on left thigh.
- Slowly squat with left leg until you feel a comfortable stretch in left calf. Keep left heel on floor.
- Pull left toes toward your shin to intensify.
- Hold for 30-60 seconds; repeat 2-3 times. Switch sides.

Note: Keep heels down and weight on back leg; lift chest and slightly arch lower back.

Straight-Knee Calf Stretch

(Stretches: Gastrocnemius)

- Step forward with right foot.
- Straighten left leg, gradually pressing left heel to floor.
- Stop when you feel a comfortable stretch in left calf.
- To intensify, pull left toes toward shin.
- Hold for 30-60 seconds; repeat 2-3 times. Switch sides.

Note: Keep your heels down and weight on back leg; lift chest and slightly arch lower back.

Resistance Tubing Exercises

One-Arm Chest Press

Muscles Worked: Pectoralis Major, Anterior Deltoid, Triceps

1. Place the door attachment at shoulder height in the door frame.
2. Your feet should be comfortably spaced, about two feet apart, with the left foot in front of the right (for stability). Keep your knees slightly bent.
3. Grip one handle (or both handles for twice the resistance) in your right hand.
4. Bring your right elbow up, just below shoulder height. Then bring your left arm up so that it is straight out in front. Make sure the tubing is taut at this point.
5. Stabilize your torso (see pg. 11) by tightening your mid-section. Hold the contraction throughout the exercise.
6. Slowly push your right arm forward and at the same time draw your left arm back. Keep pushing until your right arm is straight in front of you. Your shoulders should remain square.
7. Pause briefly in the finish position, then slowly return to the start position.
8. Repeat the exercise in a slow and controlled fashion until you have completed the set, then switch to the other side.

Incline Chest Press

Muscles Worked: Pectoralis Major, Anterior Deltoid, Triceps

1. Place the door attachment below the lower hinge in the door frame.
2. Your feet should be comfortably spaced, about two feet apart, with the left foot in front of the right (for stability). Keep your knees slightly bent.
3. Grip one handle (or both handles for twice the resistance) in your right hand.
4. Bring your right elbow up, just below shoulder height. Then bring your left arm up so that it is straight and pointed upward at a 45 degree angle in front. Make sure the tubing is taut at this point.
5. Stabilize your torso (see pg. 11) by tightening your mid-section. Hold the contraction throughout the exercise.
6. Slowly push your right arm upward and at the same time draw your left arm down. Keep pushing until your right arm straightens and is at a 45 degree angle.
7. Pause briefly in the finish position, then slowly return to the start position.
8. Repeat the exercise in a slow and controlled fashion until you have completed the set, then switch to the other side.

Downward Chest Crossover

Muscles Worked: Anterior Deltoid, Pectoralis Major

1. Place the door attachment at the top of the door frame.
2. Your feet should be comfortably spaced apart, with the left foot slightly in front of the right (for stability) and your knees slightly bent.
3. Grip one handle (or both handles for twice the resistance) in your right hand.
4. Position yourself so that your right side is toward the door, with your right arm parallel to the floor, slightly forward and straight (slight bend in the elbow). Make sure the tubing is taut.
5. Stabilize your torso (see pg. 11) by tightening your mid-section. Hold the contraction throughout the exercise.
6. Slowly bring your right arm downward and across your chest, bending slightly at the elbow as it passes in front of your chest. Do not turn or twist your torso. Your shoulders should remain square.
7. Pause briefly in the finish position, then slowly return to the start position.
8. Repeat the exercise in a slow and controlled fashion until you have completed the set, then switch to the other side.

Decline Chest Press

Muscles Worked: Anterior Deltoid, Pectoralis Major, Triceps

Start

Finish

1. Place the door attachment above the upper hinge in the door frame.
2. Your feet should be comfortably spaced, about two feet apart, with the left foot in front of the right (for stability). Keep your knees slightly bent.
3. Grip one handle (or both handles for twice the resistance) in your right hand.
4. Bring your right elbow up, just above shoulder height. Then point your left arm down so that it is straight and pointed downward at a 45 degree angle in front. Make sure the tubing is taut at this point.
5. Stabilize your torso (see pg. 11) by tightening your mid-section. Hold the contraction throughout the exercise.
6. Slowly push your right arm downward and at the same time bring your left arm up. Keep pushing until your right arm straightens and is at a 45 degree angle downward.
7. Pause briefly in the finish position, then slowly return to the start position.
8. Repeat the exercise in a slow and controlled fashion until you have completed the set, then switch to the other side.

Chest Flye

Muscles Worked: Anterior Deltoid, Pectoralis Major

Start

Finish

1. Place the door attachment at shoulder height in the door frame.
2. Your feet should be comfortably spaced, about two feet apart, with the left foot in front of the right (for stability).
3. Grip the handle in your right hand.
4. Position yourself so that your right side is toward the door, your right arm is straight out, slightly in front, and aligned with the tubing. Bend your elbow slightly and lock it in this position. Make sure the tubing is taut.
5. Stabilize your torso (see pg. 11) by tightening your mid-section. Hold the contraction throughout the exercise.
6. Slowly bring your arm straight across your chest, without bending your elbow. Do not twist or turn your torso: your shoulders must be square.
7. Pause briefly when your arm is directly in front of you, then slowly return to the start position.
8. Repeat the exercise in a slow and controlled fashion until you have completed the set, then switch to the other side.

Training Tip:

The return phase of an exercise is as important as the execution. The return should be slow and controlled.

Standing Upper Flye

Muscles Worked: Pectoralis Major, Anterior Deltoid

1. Place the door attachment at the middle hinge in the door frame.
2. Your feet should be comfortably spaced, about two feet apart, with the right foot in front of the left (for stability). Keep your knees slightly bent.
3. Griping one handle in each hand, position yourself so that your back is toward the door.
4. Hold your arms straight out to the side at shoulder level, with your elbows slightly bent and locked in this position. Make sure the tubing is taut.
5. Stabilize your torso (see pg. 11) by tightening your mid-section. Hold the contraction throughout the exercise.
6. Keeping a slight bend your elbows, slowly bring your arms towards each other until the meet in front of your chest.
7. Pause briefly in the finish position, then slowly return to the start position.
8. Repeat the exercise in a slow and controlled fashion until you have completed the set.

Standing Side Raise

Muscles Worked: Deltoid

1. Stand on the tubing, feet shoulder-width apart. Grasp the left handle in the right hand and the right handle in the left so the tubing is crossed.
2. Stabilize your torso (see pg. 11) by tightening your mid-section. Hold the contraction throughout the exercise.
3. With your arms directly at your sides and a slight bend at the elbows, slowly begin to lift your arms up and away from your body in a fluid motion.
4. Continue lifting until your arms are parallel to the floor. If you have trouble achieving parallel try a lighter resistance tube.
5. Pause briefly in the finish position, then slowly return to the start position.
6. Repeat the exercise in a slow and controlled fashion until you have completed the set.

Overhead Shoulder Press

Muscles Worked: Deltoid, Trapezius, Triceps

Start Finish

1. **Place your right foot on the tubing at the halfway mark, so that both sides are equal length.**
2. **Your feet should be comfortably spaced apart with the right foot slightly in front of the left (for stability).**
3. **Grasp the left handle in the right hand and the right handle in the left so the tubing is crossed.**
4. **Bring your hands so they are on either side of your head, with your palms facing inward. The tubing should be taut.**
5. **Stabilize your torso (see pg. 11) by tightening your mid-section. Hold the contraction throughout the exercise.**
6. **Slowly start to push upward, until your arms are almost straight. Keep a slight bend in the elbow.**
7. **Pause briefly in the upper position, then slowly return to the start position.**
8. **Repeat the exercise in a slow and controlled fashion until you have completed the set.**

TIP: To increase resistance, loop the tubing once or twice around your foot.

Single Arm Side Raise

Muscles Worked: Deltoid

Start

Finish

1. Place the door attachment below the lower hinge in the door frame.
2. Your feet should be comfortably spaced, about two feet apart. Keep your knees slightly bent.
3. Grip one handle (or both handles for twice the resistance) in your left hand.
4. Position yourself so that your right side is toward the door, your left arm is angled downward, in line with the tubing, and your hand is at the centre line of your body. Make sure the tubing is taut.
5. Stabilize your torso (see pg. 11) by tightening your mid-section. Hold the contraction throughout the exercise.
6. Bend your elbow slightly and lock it in this position so that your arm is stiff. Slowly bring your arm straight out and up from your side. Continue until your hand reaches about shoulder height.
7. Pause briefly in the extended position, then slowly return to the start position.
8. Repeat the exercise in a slow and controlled fashion until you have completed the set, then switch to the other side.

Front Deltoid Raise

Muscles Worked: Anterior Deltoid, Middle Deltoid

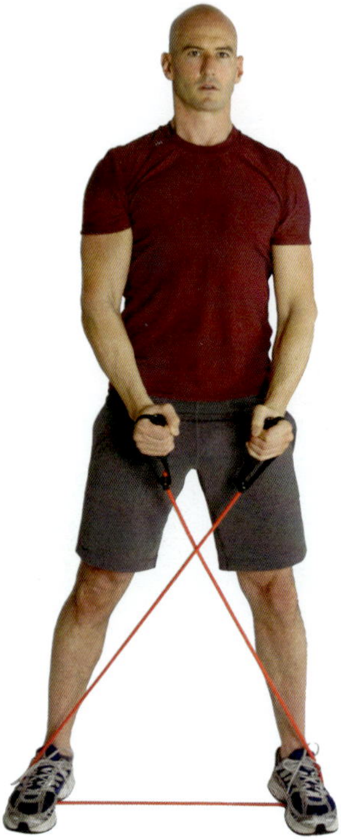

Start

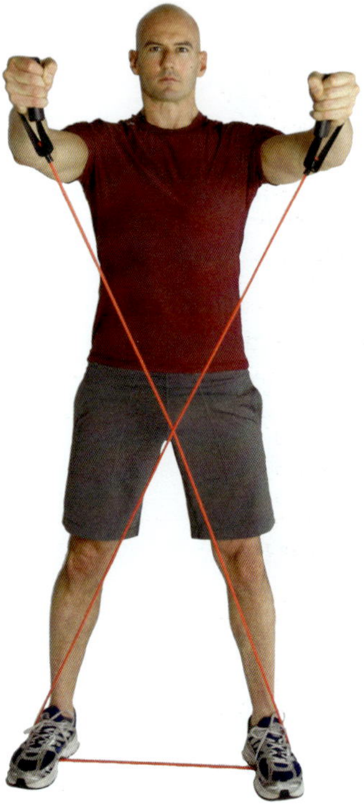

Finish

1. **Stand on the tubing, feet shoulder-width apart. Grasp the left handle in the right hand and the right handle in the left so the tubing is crossed.**
2. **Position yourself with a slight bend your knees, your palms facing inwards, holding the handles in front of your hips. Make sure the tubing is taut.**
3. **Stabilize your torso (see pg. 11) by tightening your mid-section. Hold the contraction throughout the exercise.**
4. **Keep your arms straight with a slight bend your elbow as you begin by slowly raising your arms up to shoulder level.**
5. **Pause briefly in the finish position, then slowly return to the start position.**
6. **Repeat the exercise with your right arm.**
7. **Continue in a slow and controlled fashion until you have completed the set.**

Bent-Over Flye Reverse

Muscles Worked: Posterior Deltoid, Rhomboid, Trapezius

1. Stand with your feet spaced about shoulder-width apart and the tubing running under the arches of your feet.
2. Grasp the handles so the tubing makes a cross (ie. right handle in the left hand and left handle in the right).
3. You should be slightly hunched over with your back flat. Your hands should be resting next to your knees.
4. Stabilize your torso (see pg. 11) by tightening your mid-section. Hold the contraction throughout the exercise.
5. Begin slowly moving your arms out to the sides. Your arms should be the only part that is moving.
6. Continue until your arms reach about shoulder height.
7. Pause briefly in the finish position, then slowly return to the start position.
8. Repeat the exercise in a slow and controlled fashion until you have completed the set.

Start

Finish

Standing Reverse Flye

Muscles Worked: Posterior Deltoid, Middle Deltoid Trapezius, Rhomboid

1. Place the door attachment at shoulder height in the door frame.
2. Your feet should be comfortably spaced apart and your knees slightly bent (for stability).
3. Grip the handles, one in each hand.
4. Facing the door, your arms are straight out in front and in line with the tubing. Make sure the tubing is taut.
5. Stabilize your torso (see pg. 11) by tightening your mid-section. Hold the contraction throughout the exercise.
6. Keep a slight bend in your elbows as you begin to pull your arms straight out to the sides of your body. Focus on pulling from the shoulders and not the elbows.
7. Continue through the range of motion until your hands are in line with the sides of your body.
8. Pause briefly in the finish position, then slowly return to the start position.
9. Repeat the exercise in a slow and controlled fashion until you have completed the set.

Shoulder Raise

Muscles Worked: Anterior Deltoid, Middle Deltoid, Trapezius

Start

Finish

1. Place your right foot midway along the tubing and step forward with your left leg.
2. Bend your knees and lower your hips toward the floor making sure the tubing runs evenly and securely under your right foot.
3. Grip the handles so they are on either side of your body. Make sure the tubing is taut.
4. Stabilize your torso (see pg. 11) by tightening your mid-section. Hold the contraction throughout the exercise.
5. Begin this exercise with your hands at your sides, elbows slightly bent and fixed in this position. Slowly raise your arms up and straight out in front of you. Keep your arms stiff; don't bend your elbows as you come forward.
6. Focus on using your shoulders and not elbows to raise your arms. Your hands may come together as they get higher.
7. Pause briefly when your hands reach eye level, then slowly return to the start position.
8. Repeat the exercise in a slow and controlled fashion until you have completed the set.

Forward Shoulder Press

Muscles Worked: Anterior Deltoid, Middle Deltoid, Trapezius

1. Place the door attachment just below the lower hinge in the door frame.
2. Your feet should be comfortably spaced, about two feet apart, with one foot slightly in front of the other (for stability).
3. With your back towards the door, grip a handle in each hand and bring your hands up so they are on either side of your chest, with your palms facing forward. Make sure the tubing is taut.
4. Stabilize your torso (see pg. 11) by tightening your mid-section. Hold the contraction throughout the exercise.
5. Slowly, push your arms up and out in front of you, until your arms are straight.
6. Pause briefly in the upper position, then slowly return to the start position.
7. Repeat the exercise in a slow and controlled fashion until you have completed the set.

Internal Shoulder Rotation

Muscles Worked: Pectoralis Major, Subscapularis

Start

Finish

1. Place the door attachment just above hip height in the door frame. The tubing should be at elbow height when your arm is at your side.
2. Place a rolled towel or half foam roller between your torso and your upper arm, just above the elbow.
3. Grip a handle (or both handles for twice the resistance) in your right hand. With your right side towards the door, keeping your elbow at your side, raise your hand so that your elbow is at a 90 degree angle such that your forearm is parallel to the floor and point towards the attachment. Make sure the tubing is taut.
4. Stabilize your torso (see pg. 11) by tightening your mid-section. Hold the contraction throughout the exercise.
5. Begin this exercise by slowly pivoting your forearm towards your waist. Do not twist your body. Your elbow must remain in the same position.
6. Continue until your forearm reaches your waist.
7. Pause briefly in this position, then slowly return to the start position.
8. Repeat the exercise in a slow and controlled fashion until you have completed the set.

External Shoulder Rotation

Muscles Worked: Infraspinatus, Teres Minor

Physio Tip:

The Pressure against the towel helps to secure the head of the Humerus in the Glenoi fossa (shoulder socket).

1. **Place the door attachment just above hip height in the door frame. The tubing should be at elbow height when your arm is at your side. Place a rolled towel or half foam, roller between your torso and your upper arm, just above the elbow, for added stability.**
2. **Your feet should be comfortably spaced apart.**
3. **Grip a handle (or both handles for twice the resistance) in your left hand. With your right side towards the door, keeping your elbow at your side raise your hand so that your elbow is at a 90 degree angle, such that your forearm is parallel to the floor and directly in front of you. Make sure the tubing is taut.**
4. **Stabilize your torso (see pg. 11) by tightening your mid-section. Hold the contraction throughout the exercise.**
5. **Begin this exercise by slowly pivoting your forearm away from your waist. Avoid squeezing your shoulder blades together. Your elbow must remain in the same position.**
6. **Continue until you feel a comfortable stretch in your shoulder. Don't pivot your forearm beyond the comfort range.**
7. **Pause briefly in this position, then slowly return to the start position.**
8. **Repeat the exercise in a slow and controlled fashion until you have completed the set.**

Standing Crossover

Muscles Worked: Supraspinatus, Infraspinatus, Teres Minor, Deltoid, Trapezius, Rhomboid

Start

Finish

1. Place the door attachment just below hip height in the door frame.
2. Your feet should be comfortably spaced apart, with one foot slightly in front of the other.
3. Grip a handle (or both handles for twice the resistance) in your left hand, with your right side towards the door. Your left arm should be pulled across your torso with your left hand in front of your right hip. Make sure the tubing is taut.
4. Stabilize your torso (see pg. 11) by tightening your mid-section. Hold the contraction throughout the exercise.
5. Begin this exercise by locking your elbow so that your arm is stiff, then slowly move your arm out, upward and to the left. Do not bend your elbow as you are going through this motion.
6. Continue until you feel a comfortable stretch in your shoulder. Don't rotate your forearm beyond the comfort range.
7. Pause briefly in this position, then slowly return to the start position.
8. Repeat the exercise in a slow and controlled fashion until you have completed the set.

Lying External Rotation

Muscles Worked: Infraspinatus, Teres Minor

Start

Incorrect Form

Do not bend wrist

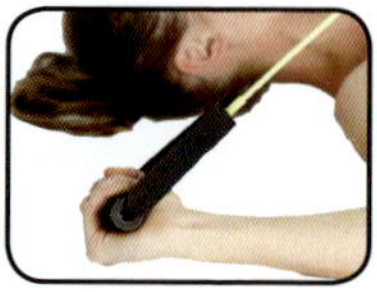

Proper Form

Finish

1. Lying on your back, wrap the tubing around your right foot and cross the handles.
2. With a handle in each hand, place your elbows on the floor at shoulder level so your upper arm and torso are at right angles.
3. Keeping a slightly bent leg, lift your right foot off the floor until your thigh is perpendicular to the floor.
4. Keeping your upper arms on the floor, bend your elbows to 90 degrees. Your lower arms are pointing straight up to the ceiling.
5. Maintaining the angle at the elbows and keeping your upper arms in place, slowly pull the handles toward the floor behind you.
6. Pause briefly in the finish position, then slowly return to the start position.
7. Repeat the exercise in a slow and controlled fashion until you have completed the set. Repeat using the other leg.

Standing Mid-Row

Muscles Worked: Latissimus Dorsi, Middle Trapezius, Rhomboid, Biceps

Start　　　　Finish

1. Place the door attachment mid level at hip height in the door frame.
2. Your feet should be comfortably spaced, about 12 inches apart, with one foot slightly in front of the other (for stability). Bend your knees slightly.
3. Grip the handles, one in each hand.
4. Facing the door, your arms are in front, straight, and angled downward in line with the tubing. Make sure the tubing is taut.
5. Stabilize your torso (see pg. 11) by tightening your mid-section. Hold the contraction throughout the exercise.
6. Begin to pull your arms backwards, bending at the elbows with your arms tucked into your sides.
7. Pause briefly when your hands reach your hips, then slowly return to the start position.
8. Repeat the exercise in a slow and controlled fashion until you have completed the set.

Training Tip:

The return phase of an exercise is as important as the execution. The return should be slow and controlled.

Standing High Pulldown

Muscles Worked: Latissimus Dorsi, Rhomboid, Posterior Deltoid, Triceps

1. Place the door attachment at the top of the door frame.
2. Your feet should be comfortably spaced apart, with the one foot in front of the other and your knees slightly bent.
3. Grip the handles, one in each hand.
4. Position yourself so that you are facing the door, your arms straight out and slightly upward, in line with the tubing. Make sure the tubing is taut.
5. Stabilize your torso (see pg. 11) by tightening your mid-section. Hold the contraction throughout the exercise.
6. Slowly start pulling the handles back and down, keeping your arms straight as they come down.
7. Pause briefly in this position, then slowly return to the start position.
8. Repeat the exercise in a slow and controlled fashion until you have completed the set.

Seated Low Row

Muscles Worked: Latissimus Dorsi, Trapezius, Rhomboid, Biceps

1. Start by sitting on the floor and wrapping the tubing around your feet (see below), so that it comes up the outside of your legs. Make sure both sides are of equal length to insure equal resistance.
2. You can increase or decrease the resistance by changing the distance between your feet (before you wrap the tubing). Bend your knees slightly.
3. Grip the left handle in the right hand and the right handle in the left so the tubing is crossed.
4. Stabilize your torso (see pg. 11) by tightening your mid-section. Hold the contraction throughout the exercise.
5. Begin to pull your arms backwards, bending at the elbows with your arms tucked into your sides.
6. Continue pulling until your hands reach your abdominal area.
7. Pause briefly in this position, then slowly return to the start position.
8. Repeat the exercise in a slow and controlled fashion until you have completed the set.

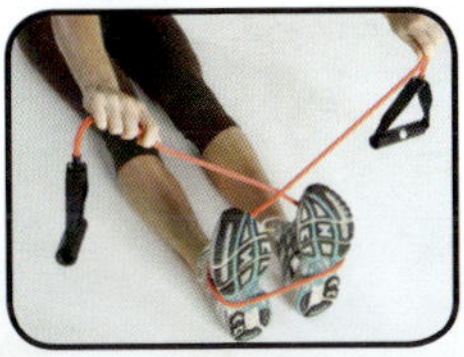

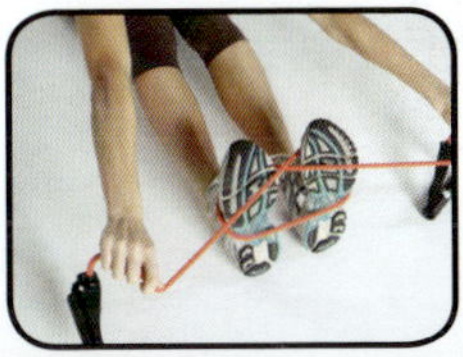

Seated High Row

Muscles Worked: Latissimus Dorsi, Rhomboid, Posterior Deltoid, Triceps

Start

Finish

1. Place the door attachment above the upper hinge in the door frame.
2. Sitting comfortably on a chair or bench, grasp the handles.
3. Position yourself so that you are facing the door, your arms straight out and angled upward, in line with the tubing. Make sure the tubing is taut.
4. Stabilize your torso (see pg. 11) by tightening your mid-section. Hold the contraction throughout the exercise.
5. Slowly, start pulling the handles back and down, bending at the elbows.
6. Bring your elbows down to your sides until your hands are slightly in front of your chest.
7. Pause briefly in this position, then slowly return to the start position.
8. Repeat the exercise in a slow and controlled fashion until you have completed the set.

Lying High Row

Muscles Worked: Posterior Deltoid, Rhomboid, Trapezius

1. Lying on your back, wrap the tubing around your right foot and cross the handles.
2. Keeping a slightly bent leg, lift your right foot off the floor until your thigh is perpendicular to the floor with a handle in each hand, straighten your arms; so they are above your upper chest and your palms are facing inward.
3. Pull the handles sideways to the floor, keeping your arms straight throughout the exercise.
4. Pause briefly in the finish position, then slowly return to the start position.
5. Repeat the exercise in a slow and controlled fashion until you have completed the set.

Training Tip:

The return phase of an exercise is as important as the execution. The return should be slow and controlled.

Half Superman Curl

Muscles Worked: Anterior Deltoid, Middle Deltoid, Gluteals, Erector Spinae

Start

Finish

1. Kneeling on a mat, place the toes of your right foot through the handle of the tubing and grip the other handle in your left hand, with the thumb at the top.
2. The tubing should run between your thighs and across your torso.
3. Position yourself on hands and knees, raising your right knee and left hand slightly off the mat.
4. Stabilize your torso (see pg. 11) by tightening your mid-section. Hold the contraction throughout the exercise.
5. Slowly and simultaneously begin raising and straightening your leg and arm. Don't let your wrist move around loosely, keep your thumb at the top and maintain that handle position throughout the motion.
6. Continue until your leg and arm are straight and in line with your back.
7. Pause, then slowly release the tension until your arm and leg are back to the starting position.
8. After completing a set on one side, switch to the other.

Standing Preacher Curl

Muscles Worked: Biceps, Brachialis, Brrachioradialis

Warning

Make sure the tubing is well attached, and that your hands are not directly in-line with your face as you pull up.

1. Place the door attachment at shoulder height in the door frame.
2. Your feet should be comfortably spaced, about a foot apart, with one in front of the other (for stability).
3. Grip the handles, one in each hand.
4. Facing the door, have your arms straight and in front of you, with your palms facing inwards. Make sure the tubing is taut.
5. Stabilize your torso (see pg. 11) by tightening your mid-section. Hold the contraction throughout the exercise.
6. Without moving your upper arms or shoulders, slowly begin to pull the handles toward you. Concentrate on keeping your elbows together as you bring your hands toward you.
7. Pause briefly when your hands are eye level, then slowly return to the start position.
8. Repeat the exercise in a slow and controlled fashion until you have completed the set.

Training Tip:

Don't hold your breath. Exhale on exertion and inhale on the return.

Standing Bicep Curl

Muscles Worked: Biceps, Brachialis, Brachioradialis

1. Place your right foot on the tubing at the halfway mark, so that both sides are equal length.
2. Your feet should be comfortably spaced apart with the right foot slightly in front of the right.
3. Grip a handle in each hand and bend your knees slightly.
4. Begin with your palms facing inwards with your hands at your sides. The tubing should be taut.
5. Stabilize your torso (see pg. 11) by tightening your mid-section. Hold the contraction throughout the exercise.
6. Bending the elbows, keep your upper arms fixed at your sides as you bring your hands up.
7. Pause briefly in the upper position, then slowly return to the start position.
8. Repeat the exercise in a slow and controlled fashion until you have completed the set.

Training Tip:

To increase resistance, loop the tubing once or twice around your foot.

Overhead Extension

Muscles Worked: Triceps

Start   Finish

1. Place your right foot on the tubing at the halfway mark, so that both sides are equal length.
2. Your feet should be comfortably spaced apart with the right foot slightly behind the left (for stability).
3. Grip the handles one in each hand and position your hands comfortably behind your neck with your elbows pointing towards the ceiling. Make sure the tubing is taut.
4. Stabilize your torso (see pg. 11) by tightening your midsection. Hold the contraction throughout the exercise.
5. Keeping your shoulders and upper arms in a fixed position, begin straightening your arms upward until your hands are directly above you. Try to keep your elbows together throughout the motion.
6. Pause briefly when your arms are almost straight, then slowly return to the start position.
7. Repeat the exercise in a slow and controlled fashion until you have completed the set.

Tricep Pulldown

Muscles Worked: Triceps

Start

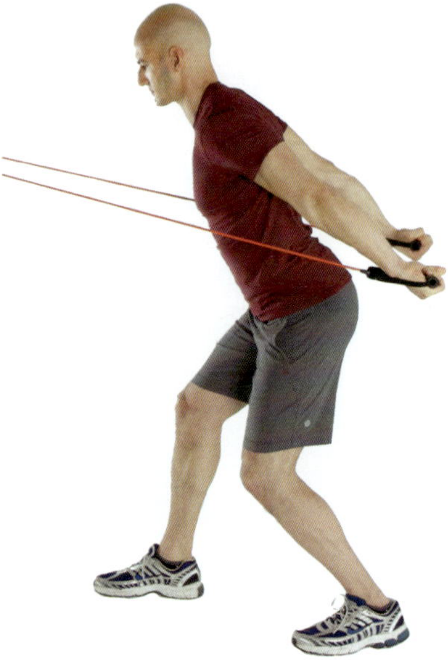

Finish

1. Place the door attachment at the top of the door frame.
2. Your feet should be comfortably spaced, about 12 inches apart, with one foot slightly in front of the other (for stability). Bend your knees slightly.
3. Grip the handles, one in each hand.
4. Stabilize your torso (see pg. 11) by tightening your mid-section. Hold the contraction throughout the exercise.
5. Facing the door, place your elbows to your sides. Make sure the tubing is taut.
6. Keeping your elbows at your side, begin by straightening your arms downward, until they are straight.
7. Pause briefly in the finish position, then slowly return to the start position.
8. Repeat the exercise in a slow and controlled fashion until you have completed the set.

Wrist Curl & Reverse Wrist Curl

Muscles Worked: Wrist Flexors, Finger Flexors, (Reverse-Wrist Extensors)

Start **REVERSE** Finish

1. Sit comfortably on the seat with your feet spread slightly wider than shoulder width apart.
2. Wrap the tubing around your left foot and grip one of the handles in your right hand. The shorter and/or tighter the tubing between your hand and foot, the greater the resistance.

   REVERSE: Wrap the tubing around your right foot and grip the handle in your right hand.
3. With your right palm facing up, hold the handle in your curled fingers. Your right elbow should be resting comfortably on your right leg. The tubing should be taut.

   REVERSE: With your right palm facing downward, hold the handle in your curled fingers. Your right elbow should be resting comfortably on your right leg, with your wrist slightly over your knee.
4. Relax your wrist so that the handle is in the lower position.
5. Bring the handle upward with your hand until your wrist is completely flexed.

   REVERSE: Bring the handle upward by bending your wrist back. Keep your forearm in contact with your thigh throughout
6. Slowly lower the handle back to the start position.

Crunch

Muscles Worked: Rectus Abdominis, Obliques

Start

Finish

1. Place the door attachment below the lower hinge in the door frame.
2. Lie down on a mat with your head closest to the door.
3. Grip one handle in each hand. Keep your arms straight with a slight bend at the elbows. Your hands should be beside your hips. Make sure the tubing is taut.
4. Slowly begin to lift your shoulders off the mat, at the same time pushing your hands toward your feet. To create this motion, your abdominal muscles must contract.
5. Pause briefly when you feel a good contraction in the abs, then slowly return to the start position.
6. Repeat the exercise in a slow and controlled fashion until you have completed the set.

Training Tip:

Don't hold your breath. Exhale on exertion and inhale on the return.

Standing One-Arm Row

Muscles Worked: Posterior Deltoid, Obliques, Erector Spinae

1. **Place the door attachment below the lower hinge in the door frame.**
2. **Your feet should be comfortably spaced, about two feet apart, with the right foot slightly in front of the left (for stability). Bend your knees slightly.**
3. **Grip the handle in your left hand.**
4. **Facing the door, bend forward slightly from the waist. Place your right hand on your right knee for support. Your left arm should be straight and in line with the tubing. Make sure the tubing is taut.**
5. **Stabilize your torso (see pg. 11) by tightening your mid-section. Hold the contraction throughout the exercise.**
6. **Begin to pull your arm straight back and up at a constant angle.**
7. **Pause briefly when your elbow is at its highest point, then slowly return to the start position. Maintain the same angle throughout the motion.**
8. **Repeat the exercise in a slow and controlled fashion until you have completed the set, then repeat on the other side.**

Training Tip:

The return phase of an exercise is as important as the execution. The return should be slow and controlled.

Standing Side Bend

Muscles Worked: Rectus Abdominis, Obliques, Latissimus Dorsi

1. Place the door attachment at the top of the door frame.
2. Your feet should be comfortably spaced apart, with one foot slightly in front of the other and your knees slightly bent.
3. Grip one handle (or both handles for twice the resistance) in your hands.
4. Position yourself so that your right side is toward the door, your arms straight up and hands clasped together. Make sure the tubing is taut when you begin.
5. Stabilize your torso (see pg. 11) by tightening your mid-section. Hold the contraction throughout the exercise.
6. Slowly, by bending at your left side, bring your arms down and away from the door. Your arms should remain fixed and above your head.
7. Pause briefly in the finish position, then slowly return to the start position.
8. Repeat the exercise in a slow and controlled fashion until you have completed the set, then switch to the other side.

Standing Side Twist (arms bent)

Muscles Worked: Obliques, Rectus Abdominis

1. **Place the door attachment at shoulder height in the door frame.**
2. **Your feet should be comfortably spaced apart, with one foot slightly in front of the other and your knees slightly bent.**
3. **Grip both handles in your hands.**
4. **Position yourself so that your right side is toward the door. Your arms are bent with your hand toward the right shoulder. Make sure the tubing is taut.**
5. **Stabilize your torso (see pg. 11) by tightening your mid-section. Hold the contraction throughout the exercise.**
6. **Slowly twist away from the door, keeping your arms braced in the same position.**
7. **Pause briefly in the finish position, then slowly return to the start position.**
8. **Repeat the exercise in a slow and controlled fashion until you have completed the set, then switch to the other side.**

Standing Side Twist (arms straight)

Muscles Worked: Obliques

1. Place the door attachment at shoulder height in the door frame.
2. Your feet should be comfortably spaced apart, with the right foot slightly in front of the left and your knees slightly bent.
3. Grip one handle (or both handles for twice the resistance) in both hands.
4. Position yourself so that your right side is toward the door and your arms are straight out in front. Make sure the tubing is taut.
5. Stabilize your torso (see pg. 11) by tightening your mid-section. Hold the contraction throughout the exercise.
6. Slowly twist away from the door, keeping your arms braced in the same position. Bend slightly forward as you turn at the waist to increase the resistance.
7. Pause briefly in the finish position, then slowly return to the start position.
8. Repeat the exercise in a slow and controlled fashion until you have completed the set, then switch to the other side.

Twisting Trunk Crunch

Muscles Worked: Obliques, Rectus Abdominis

Start

Finish

1. Place the door attachment below the lower hinge in the door frame.
2. Lie down on a mat with your head closest to the door.
3. Grip one handle (or both handles for twice the resistance in your left hand.
4. Pull the tubing down towards your pelvic area. Keep you arm straight with a slight bend at the elbow. Your left hand should be at your right hip bone. Make sure the tubing is taut.
5. Stabilize your torso (see pg. 11) by tightening your midsection. Hold the contraction throughout the exercise.
6. Slowly begin lifting your left shoulder off the mat; at the same time, push your hand forward past your right hip. To create this motion, your abdominal muscles must contract.
7. Pause briefly when you feel a good contraction in the abs, then slowly return to the start position
8. Repeat the exercise in a slow and controlled fashion until you have completed the set, then switch to the other side.

Reverse Wood Chop

Muscles Worked: Obliques, Rectus Abdominis, Deltoids, Erector Spinae

1. Place your right foot on the tubing at the halfway mark, so that both sides are equal length.
2. Your feet should be comfortably spaced, about 12 inches apart, with one foot slightly in front of the other (for stability). Bend your knees slightly.
3. Grip both handles with both hands.
4. Start with your shoulders slightly rotated towards your right foot and your arms are angled downward and in line with the tubing. Make sure the tubing is taut.
5. Stabilize your torso (see pg. 11) by tightening your mid-section. Hold the contraction throughout the exercise.
6. Begin to pull your arms to the left in an arc-type motion, keeping your arms straight and stiff. Your weight should shift to the left leg.
7. Pause briefly when your hands are above your head, then slowly return to the starting position and repeat the exercise to the right side.
8. Continue in a slow and controlled fashion until you have completed the set.

Kneeling Oblique Crunch

Muscles Worked: Obliques, Rectus Abdominis

1. Place the door attachment just above the upper door hinge.
2. Kneel sideways to the door and grip the handle with both hands.
3. Hold your arms out straight and rotate your torso towards the door until your arms are running in line with the tubing. Bend forward slightly at the hips.
4. Stabilize your torso (see pg. 11) by tightening your mid-section. Hold the contraction throughout the exercise.
5. Start the exercise by slowly rotating your shoulders down and towards the opposite knee. The movement should come from a contraction in the abdominals.
6. Pause briefly when you feel a good contraction in the abs, then slowly return to the start position.
7. Repeat the exercise in a slow and controlled fashion until you have completed the set. Then repeat on the other side.

Training Tip:

Don't hold your breath. Exhale on exertion and inhale on the return.

Training Tip:

The return phase of an exercise is as important as the execution. The return should be slow and controlled.

Seated Ankle Eversion

Muscles Worked: Peroneals

Start

Finish

1. Sitting upright on the floor, straighten your legs and place your feet together.
2. Run the tubing under your feet, just below the toes. Then bring the tubing back over the top of the feet and loop the right one under the left foot and the left one under the right foot so that they are crossed in the middle.
3. Pull the tubing taut on the outside of the feet.
4. Slowly spread your feet apart at the toes, keeping your heels together and on the ground.
5. Pause briefly when the tops of your feet are about 6 inches apart, then slowly return to the start position.
6. Continue in a slow and controlled fashion until you have completed the set.

Squat

Muscles Worked: Quadriceps, Gluteus Maximus, Hamstrings

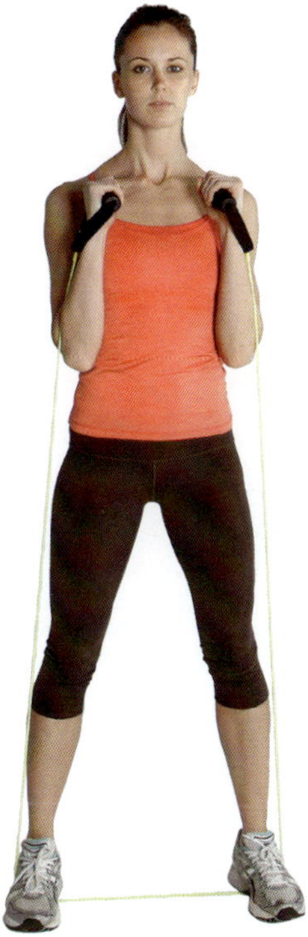

Start

Finish

Side View

1. **Grip a handle in each hand. Stand on the mid-point of the tubing so that the distance from foot to handle is the same on both sides.**
2. **Bring your arms up so that the tubing runs behind your arms, palms facing inwards, and your hands are in front of your shoulders.**
3. **Stand upright, knees slightly bent, your feet shoulder-width apart.**
4. **Stabilize your torso (see pg. 11) by tightening your mid-section. Hold the contraction throughout the exercise.**
5. **Slowly lower your hips until your upper thighs are almost parallel to the floor. Try not to let your knees extend past the toes as you come down. Keep your head level to the ground. Your arms remain in the same position throughout.**
6. **Pause at the bottom and slowly return to the standing position, straightening your legs and hips at the same time.**
7. **Keep your back flat or with a slight arch throughout the exercise.**
8. **Keep your feet firmly on the floor and squat only as low as you can with proper technique. Use light resistance tubing or no resistance the first time you perform this exercise.**

Split Squat

Muscles Worked: Quadriceps, Gluteus Maximus, Hamstrings

Start Finish

1. Grip a handle in each hand. Stand shoulder width at the mid point of the tubing, so that the distance from foot to handle is the same on both sides. Step forward with your left foot.
2. Bring your arms up so that the tubing runs down the outside of your arms, your palms facing inward, elbows together, and your hands at shoulder level.
3. Stand with your feet spaced about 3-4 feet apart, one in front of the other. Keep your back straight and your head level with the floor throughout.
4. Stabilize your torso (see pg. 11) by tightening your mid-section. Hold the contraction throughout the exercise.
5. Slowly drop your hips until your back knee nearly touches the floor.
6. Pause for a moment, then slowly push yourself back to the starting position.
7. Do not bend your front knee beyond 90 degrees or let it pass beyond your toes.
8. Continue in a slow and controlled fashion until you have completed the set, then repeat with the other leg.

Foot Curl

Muscles Worked: Tibialis Anterior, Peroneals, Extensor Digitorum Longus

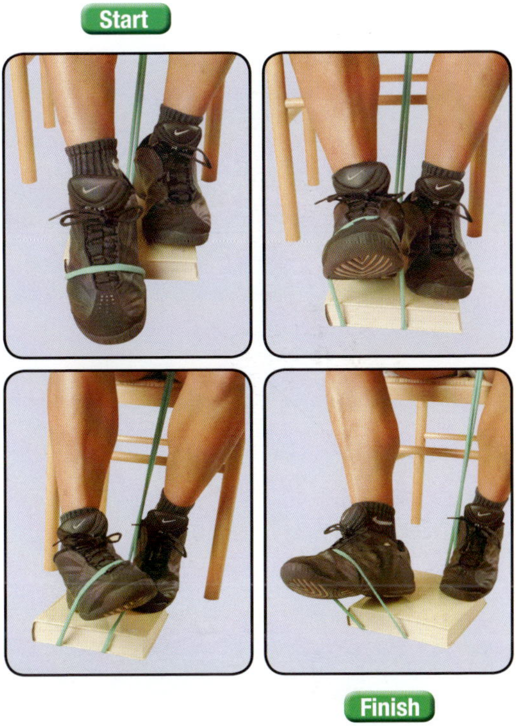

1. For this exercise, you need an old textbook, preferably an inch to two inches thick.
2. Place the textbook on the tubing so that a loop just big enough to fit the top of your foot is sticking out beyond the front of the textbook.
3. Place your right foot in the loop and secure the tubing by pressing down on the top of the textbook with your left foot. Make sure the tubing is taut.
4. Slowly lift the top of your foot straight up using your heel as the pivot point: your heel remains on the book.
5. Then slowly move your foot to the right, then the left, and finally back to the starting position.
6. Continue in a slow and controlled fashion until you have completed the set.

Leg Extension

Muscles Worked: Quadriceps

1. **Lying on your back, wrap the tubing around your right foot and hook the left handle onto your left foot. Hold the other handle in your left hand.**
2. **Keeping your right leg straight, bend the knee of the left leg to 90 degrees and make sure the upper left leg is straight up and down.**
3. **Grip your left thigh just under the knee with both hands to help stabilize your upper right leg.**
4. **Slowly straighten your left knee, while keeping your thigh fixed in the same position. In the finish position your left leg should be pointing straight up to the ceiling.**
5. **Pause briefly in the finish position, then slowly return to the start position.**
6. **Repeat the exercise in a slow and controlled fashion until you have completed the set, then switch to the other side.**

Seated Leg Abduction

Muscles Worked: External Hip Rotators

1. **Sitting upright on the edge of a chair, place your feet together.**
2. **With your knees together, wrap the tubing around your legs, just above the knees. Make sure the tubing is taut.**
3. **Begin by slowly spread your legs apart at the knees, keeping your feet together. If the tubing causes you any discomfort, try wearing sweat pants or draping a towel over your thighs.**
4. **Pause briefly when your knees are about a foot apart, then slowly return to the start position.**
5. **If you feel any strain on the knees, you should bring your knees closer together. Concentrate on maintaining upright posture.**
6. **Continue in a slow and controlled fashion until you have completed the set.**